LIFE IS A POEM

LIFE IS A POEM

THE SIGHS OF LIFE:
EXPRESSING THE MOMENTS OF THE SOUL

TUESE C. AHKIONG

iUniverse, Inc.
Bloomington

LIFE IS A POEM
THE SIGHS OF LIFE:
EXPRESSING THE MOMENTS OF THE SOUL

Through out this book Bible passages are used from the NASB, NIV and ESV.

NASB (New American Standard Bible (NASB) Copyright © 1960, 1962, 1963, 1968, 1971, 1972, 1973, 1975, 1977, 1995 by The Lockman Foundation),
NIV (New International Version 1984 (NIV1984)) and Copyright © 1973, 1978, 1984 by Biblica
ESV (The Holy Bible, English Standard Version Copyright © 2001 by Crossway Bibles, a division of Good News Publishers).

iUniverse books may be ordered through booksellers or by contacting:

iUniverse
1663 Liberty Drive
Bloomington, IN 47403
www.iuniverse.com
1-800-Authors (1-800-288-4677)

Because of the dynamic nature of the Internet, any web addresses or links contained in this book may have changed since publication and may no longer be valid. The views expressed in this work are solely those of the author and do not necessarily reflect the views of the publisher, and the publisher hereby disclaims any responsibility for them.

Any people depicted in stock imagery provided by Thinkstock are models, and such images are being used for illustrative purposes only.
Certain stock imagery © Thinkstock.

ISBN: 978-1-4620-5995-9 (sc)
ISBN: 978-1-4620-6024-5 (ebk)

Printed in the United States of America

iUniverse rev. date: 10/27/2011

ACKNOWLEDGEMENTS

I would first like to thank my beautiful sister, Upuia (Pooh) for encouraging me to share my creativity in the form of this book. She has been such a support in bringing "Life is a Poem" to life. I have wanted to compile this book for years but have procrastinated. In 2010, she challenged me to set a goal of putting my creative expressions into a book. This is just the catalyst I needed to get on the ball.

I thank my mama, Vineta Ahkiong, for being a good, loving and encouraging mother. She has always been in my corner supporting me in all my endeavors. My mother has blessed me with a love for music and song. I remember her singing to me as a little guy. My mom has lived a hard life and singing praises to The Lord on her ukulele has been her oasis. Mom would find strength, joy and delight from God's presence, as she would worship Him. Her example has been a blessing to me.

It's amazing how life changes when meeting certain people. I am grateful to a good old friend, Glenn Dalmacio for being there for me back in 1990 during a break-up I went through. He is a poet and suggested that I journal about my experiences. He also inspired me to write poetry as I found listening to his work to be a soothing remedy to my blues. At first, writing was a therapy of sorts to cope with my circumstances. Later, after getting over that chapter in life, I found a new passion and friend, my pen.

Well, I suppose I have to thank my first girlfriend for the break-up. God in His Providence used this circumstance to trigger a flood of emotions that tossed me in many directions. These events humbled me. Thanks to some friends who were there for me, I was able to funnel these powerful feelings into a positive creative outlet.

I praise, worship and thank The Lord Jesus Christ. He is my Sustainer, Provider, Protector, Comforter, Deliverer, Passion, and Joy. He is The One that gives me health, strength, wisdom, creativity, restoration, vision, righteousness, peace, hope, faith, love, forgiveness, salvation and the ability to glorify Him through writing. The Lord is the Maker and Creator of all things. He makes and gives all of nature to us to enjoy, sing and write about. He also has made everyday of our life with all the many different moments: joys, pains, successes, sorrows, achievements, and even set backs. The Lord is my joy and the very reason I live and breathe.

Here are just a few Bible verses that share God's greatness in all circumstances:

For by him all things were created: things in heaven and on earth, visible and invisible, whether thrones or powers or rulers or authorities; all things were created by him and for him. He is before all things, and in him all things hold together.
Colossians 1:16-17

The heavens declare the glory of God; the skies proclaim the work of his hands.
Psalm 19:1

And we know that God causes all things to work together for good to those who love God, to those who are called according to His purpose.
Romans 8:28

I love these passages because they teach that everything is working for God's glory, purposes, and for the ultimate good of His people. Thank You, Lord, for authoring salvation in this man's life. Please use this book to extend your glory and to increase the fame of Jesus' Name. And may Your Holy Spirit minister to many hearts.

Soli Deo Gloria!
To God Alone Be The Glory!

TUESE C. AHKIONG

INTRODUCTION

My sister Upuia has been a big encouragement and motivator in bringing this book to life. I have always thought of putting some of my poems in a book but just never got around to it. She's been my catalyst to move me to action, set goals, and provide good feedback. Thank you again my sista!

It's been my desire to share my written, musical and visual art. Some of my work has blessed others and I would hate for all this creativity that God has granted me to just die with me. Perhaps there will be something in this collection of expressions that will speak to someone's heart a smile, a new perspective, an inspiration, a blessing or a sigh of life.

WHO AM I?
what makes this person me?
am I my ethnicity?
If you don't know who you are, then who do you ask?
am I a collection of what I do?
am I my job?
am I my hobbies?
am I my passions?
do my genetics determine who I am?
am I a product of my environment?

Am I my family? I am the youngest of four. The eldest is my strong and comical brother, Larry. Next in line is my wonderful beautiful sister, Tina. And the one next in age to me is Upuia whom I have mentioned already. My father is Tuese, Sr. or "Master Chef Joe" and he is half Samoan and half Chinese. My sweet musical mama, Vineta, is full Samoan.

Tuese is a Samoan name. Tu means "to stand" and ese means "away, differently or alone." So there are 3 possible meanings: To stand away, To stand differently or To stand alone. Ahkiong is a misspelled Chinese name. The story goes like this. My Grandfather Chan Tin Cheung was in immigration and his pronunciation of Cheung came out "Ah Key ong." Usually Chinese people jump start their talking with "ah . . ." and then speak their words. So, in the case of my grandfather, his annunciation was interpreted as "Ahkiong." I do not

TUESE C. AHKIONG

know what Cheung means nor Chang. Why Chang? On my birth certificate, Cheung which was typed but crossed through in ink with a line and Chang is written above.

This question of "Who am I?" is deeply spiritual, philosophical and religious. It's related to a whole bunch of other Ultimate Questions:

Who am I?
Where did I come from?
Where did the universe come from?
Has the universe existed forever?
Does God or gods exist?
If God exists, how can I know He exists?
Does Truth exist?
Is Truth absolute or is it relative?
Why am I the way I am?
How should I live?
Where am I going when I die?
Do humans have a soul?
What happens after death?

If one has not wrestled with these questions, then a mind has been wasted on him or her. How one answers these ultimate questions of life will influence, if not determine how one lives out their life.

LIFE IS A POEM is a collection of Tuese Ahkiong's favorite poems, doodles, photos and songs. It's a little window into some of the chapters in his life. Included are Bible verses from the ultimate Poet Himself, God. The Scriptural passages relate to these different inspirational moments and shower them with divine truth. Tuese likes to call these special occasions, **"The Sighs of Life"** because they have romanced him to write of the moment. He also feels a duty and obligation to compose for the soul of man in hopes that his words will resonate life, pleasure and enlightenment. This book is a collage of Ahkiong's early poems about life, death, love, dumps, romance, purpose, funk, controversy, transformation, depression, salvation, worship and song. Each poem will be followed by some thoughts about its motivation, circumstance and origin. There are many great experiences that one can connect with as these expressions help move the soul to know that life is a poem.

SOME BIBLE VERSES ON HOW ONE'S LIFE IS LIKE A POEM

But thanks be to God, who always leads us in triumph in Christ, and manifests through us the sweet aroma of the knowledge of Him in every place. For we are a fragrance of Christ to God among those who are being saved and among those who are perishing; to the one an aroma from death to death, to the other an aroma from life to life. And who is adequate for these things? For we are not like many, peddling the word of God, but as from sincerity, but as from God, we speak in Christ in the sight of God.

Are we beginning to commend ourselves again? Or do we need, as some, letters of commendation to you or from you? YOU ARE OUR LETTER, written in our hearts, known and read by all men; being manifested that YOU ARE A LETTER OF CHRIST, cared for by us, WRITTEN NOT WITH INK BUT WITH THE SPIRIT OF THE LIVING GOD, not on tablets of stone but on tablets of human hearts.
2 Corinthians 2:14-17, 3:1-3

Your eyes saw my unformed body. All the days ordained for me were WRITTEN IN YOUR BOOK BEFORE ONE OF THEM CAME TO BE.
Psalms 139:16

For WE ARE GOD'S WORKMANSHIP, created in Christ Jesus to do good works, which God prepared in advance for us to do.
Ephesians 2:10

Let us fix our eyes on Jesus, THE AUTHOR AND PERFECTER OF OUR FAITH, who for the joy set before him endured the cross, scorning its shame, and sat down at the right hand of the throne of God.
Hebrew 12:2

O LORD, you have searched me and you know me. You know when I sit and when I rise; you perceive my thoughts from afar. You discern my going out and my lying down; you are familiar with all my ways. Before a word is on my tongue you know it completely, O LORD. You hem me in—behind and before; you have laid your hand upon me. Such knowledge is too wonderful for me, too lofty for me to attain.
Ps 139:1-6

The plans of the heart belong to man, But the answer of the tongue is from the LORD.
Proverbs 16:1

The LORD has made everything for its own purpose, Even the wicked for the day of evil.
Proverbs 16:4

The mind of man plans his way, But the LORD directs his steps.
Proverbs 16:9

Many plans are in a man's heart, But the counsel of the LORD will stand.
Proverbs 19:21

Man's steps are ordained by the LORD, How then can man understand his way?
Proverbs 20:24

"But He is unique, and who can make Him change? And whatever His soul desires, that He does. For He performs what is appointed for me, And many such things are with Him. That is why I am

terrified before him; when I think of all this, I fear him. God has made my heart faint; the Almighty has terrified me.
Job 23:13-14

Since his days are determined, The number of his months is with You; You have appointed his limits, so that he cannot pass.
Job 14:5

, "and He made from one, every nation of mankind to live on all the face of the earth, having determined their appointed times, and the boundaries of their habitation,"
Acts 17:26

The word of the LORD came to me, saying, "Before I formed you in the womb I knew you, before you were born I set you apart; I appointed you as a prophet to the nations."
Jeremiah 1:4-5

I know, O LORD, that a man's way is not in himself, Nor is it in a man who walks to direct his steps.
Jeremiah 10:23

Who is there who speaks and it comes to pass, Unless the Lord has commanded it?
Lamentations 3:37

And now it's time to bare the soul . . .

WORDS

with my hand ready to speak
in sunny blue ink
scribbled across white paper skies
can you envision what my heart thinks?
listen and see,
what's stirring inside me
pretty pictures sing of thee
the very thought of you
does things to he
who guides this pen's
every intention
watch as my soul
flows
over,
what words can never express
that passion covered from sight
now undressed
in the light
hear,
how near
you've touched me
I spill my heart in ink
naked is what I think
before your pretty eyes alone
for only you can see me
on blue streaks
only you can hear me
on white paper sheets.
and if it's my voice
you hear,
collapse the distance
between us,
my dear
and
draw near . . .

*This is a piece I created to open-up my open mic event, The Spoken Word Slamma Jamma.

TUESE C. AHKIONG

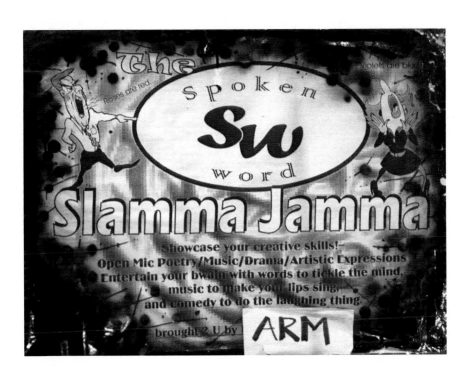

HAPPY BIRTHDAY BABY

Friends and family gather near
On your special day
To celebrate with lots of cheer
Is why we're here to say

Happy birthday baby
May all your wishes come true
Happy birthday baby
God made this day for you

So make a wish
And blow out your candles
I'll give you a kiss
That's more than you can handle

My sweet (my sweet)
My dear (my dear)
For you another year
So precious are these memories
We'll have of you today
To cherish and remember
Whenever we say

Happy birthday baby
May all your wishes come true
Happy birthday baby
God made this day for you.

Happy birthday baby
May all your wishes come true.
Wishing you a happy birthday
And a I love you.

*Happy Birthday Baby was first a poem. I later made it sing an acappella doowop, r&b and oldies jam to serenade birthday celebrants. ;-) And with the birth of "Life is a Poem" I would like to say and sing Happy Birthday Baby!

TUESE C. AHKIONG

SOME LOVE AND ROMANCE BIBLE VERSES

Let him kiss me with the kisses of his mouth—
for your love is more delightful than wine.
Pleasing is the fragrance of your perfumes;
your name is like perfume poured out.
No wonder the maidens love you!
Take me away with you—let us hurry!
Let the king bring me into his chambers.

My lover is mine and I am his;
he browses among the lilies.
Until the day breaks
and the shadows flee,
turn, my lover,
and be like a gazelle
or like a young stag
on the rugged hills.

You have stolen my heart, my sister, my bride;
you have stolen my heart
with one glance of your eyes,
with one jewel of your necklace.
How delightful is your love, my sister, my bride!
How much more pleasing is your love than wine,
and the fragrance of your perfume than any spice!
Your lips drop sweetness as the honeycomb, my bride;
milk and honey are under your tongue.
The fragrance of your garments is like that of Lebanon.
You are a garden locked up, my sister, my bride;
you are a spring enclosed, a sealed fountain.
I have taken off my robe—
must I put it on again?
I have washed my feet—
must I soil them again?

My lover thrust his hand through the latch-opening;
my heart began to pound for him.
I arose to open for my lover,
and my hands dripped with myrrh,
my fingers with flowing myrrh,
on the handles of the lock.
I opened for my lover,
but my lover had left; he was gone.
My heart sank at his departure.
I looked for him but did not find him.
I called him but he did not answer.

My lover has gone down to his garden,
to the beds of spices,
to browse in the gardens
and to gather lilies.
I am my lover's and my lover is mine;
he browses among the lilies.

How beautiful you are and how pleasing,
O love, with your delights!
Your stature is like that of the palm,
and your breasts like clusters of fruit.
I said, "I will climb the palm tree;
I will take hold of its fruit."
May your breasts be like the clusters of the vine,
the fragrance of your breath like apples,
and your mouth like the best wine.
May the wine go straight to my lover,
flowing gently over lips and teeth.

Place me like a seal over your heart,
like a seal on your arm;
for love is as strong as death,
its jealousy unyielding as the grave.
It burns like blazing fire,
like a mighty flame.

TUESE C. AHKIONG

Many waters cannot quench love;
rivers cannot wash it away.
If one were to give
all the wealth of his house for love,
it would be utterly scorned.
**Song of Solomon 1:2-4, 2:16-17, 4:9-12, 5: 3-6, 6:2-3, 7:6-10,
8:6-7**

Love is patient, love is kind.
It does not envy, it does not boast, it is not proud.
It is not rude, it is not self-seeking,
it is not easily angered, it keeps no record of wrongs.
Love does not delight in evil but rejoices with the truth.
It always protects, always trusts, always hopes, always perseveres.
Love never fails . . .
1 Corinthians 13:4-8

THE BREATH OF LOVE

lips
too close
suffocate
in breathless
conversation
breathing
words
unheard of
with breathy voices
gasping for air
supplied
by stolen breaths
that breathe
kisses
from breath-taking
positions
have no need
of a breather
or break
because a life
is at stake.
your mouth on mine,
a sort of CPR
our hearts are pumping
by simply supplying
the breath of love.

*I remember being fascinated, and even fixated on "a breath" and
the power it could supply in so many ways.

TUESE C. AHKIONG

THAT'S LOVE

It's about love
That thing that poets write of ...
That thing that changes your life,
Or better yet, gives you life.
That thing that makes your heart sing,
Tingly feelings it brings.

Just the thought of your special treasure,
Gives the most incredible pleasure.
It injects a natural narcotic high
Gives you the ummms ...
As you breathe a happy sigh.

Mooshie, Corny, sappy talk,
Starry eyes and drunken walk.
Silly words come off your lips
Honey Bunny,
Coochie Coo,
Baby Girl,
Big Daddy,
You're my world.

But that's not all,
It makes you dumb,
You say, "Two plus four, equals one."
Gaga thinking blinds you to see,
That you make stupid decisions,
Like "Drinks are on me!"

You also go crazy,
Doing things you never thought you
Would or could or should.
Rollercoaster rides
Crazy highs.

Love makes you into an athlete:
Run a thousand miles,
Swim the widest ocean,
Climb the highest mountain,
Jump over any obstacle
Just to get to your fix.

Rugged, rough and tough man
Giving up Eskimo kisses at her command.
Kind, gentle and pleasant lady
Gone Ramba nuts and berserker crazy,
When seeing him speaking with another lady.

Then there's losing sleep and sheep
Because you can't stop thinking
about your sweet.
So you lose track of counting those lambs and wham!
You get slammed with drama-rama.

But there's still more,
You get poor.
Because of one's honey,
You run out of money.
An expensive fix,
For the sweetest high,
To be apart from your sweetie pie
You would die.
That's what some call love.

*This piece was motivated from the drama-rama of many real life
experiences.

TUESE C. AHKIONG

THE GLANCE

I hunger for the very chance
That our eyes may meet
Exchange an innocent glance
Quenching my soul's thirst full.
I swim in a sea of blue
Floating free,
Carried by moonlight
With open eyes,
I cast my sight upon you
You turn my way
And catch my stare
Our eyes lock, embrace
I am hypnotized, mesmerized, in a trance.
Feeling only the warmth,
From the soft beauty of your face.
Whoever you may be,
You capture me.
I surrender the moment to you, to us.
Nothing else in time or space exist or have importance
As together our souls dance
For that breath we lived an eternity
Caught in this gaze
My every thought you possess
For your eyes pierce through me
They glimpse into my heart's windows
And know I am yours.
A play or words may make you mine,
But your stare tells all my answers.
I watch and see no lie
In our spell we speak,
But without words,
A language unique between us,
How thrilling, seductive, and crafty this game.
In mere seconds,
My feelings are offered to you.
But then as quickly as it began,

In shyness you turn away.
You leave me cold and alone
Flying blind through a sky of gray
To dance a glance another day.

*I would like to dedicate this piece to the powerful hypnotizing beauty of all the incredibly gorgeous ladies that have commanded inspiration from this man's pen.

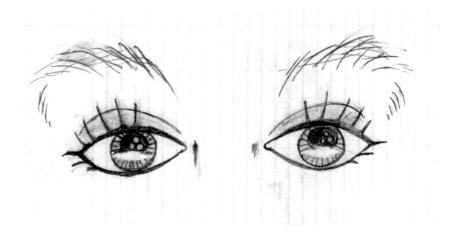

TUESE C. AHKIONG

A THROAT GULPING MOMENT

She smiles in my direction
A hair raising,
Breath taking,
Throat gulping moment.
As the tingling and jingling die down
I shy my view around.
Unfound by her.
So, do I dare?
Permit her to hold me in her stare?
Her loveliness has a way
Of making one feel sweetly uncomfortable.
I'm not just talking about us guys!
This gorgeous sight is such a pleasant delight.
What a distraction, this attraction, her beauty brings.
I'm like in a Star Wars tractor beam.
Her presence has a way of pulling my glance
Upon her.
Suspended in the touch
Of her presence.
How it commands me!
Understand me!
Whenever she's near me,
My fullest attention
She has of me.
For I am . . .
. . . gaga,
Floating free and whooped.
Somewhere in the air,
Lost beneath her hair.
Right there,
Falling,
In her eyes,
Downward towards her heart,
Longing to be a part,
That's vital in need,
A necessity.

More than air,
That cares for the flesh.
A breath of love,
That captures her forever affection
And keeps her starry eyes in my direction.

*This piece describes all those sweet awkward feeling of gazing
upon a beauty.

A MAUI NIGHT

I watch as streaks of moonlight
Lick the face of the ocean wet.
She sighs with each touch
And i hear the gentle rumble
Of navy blue sea,
Clashing with
Night light rays
Of electricity.
With starry wishy skies
And you by my side,
Mother nature has done it again,
Setting the mood for free,
With no need
Of artificial flavors or preservatives,
Neither words, nor Sinatra.
The soothing sound of the soft sea
Sings a slow song ballad for us.
We find our souls dancing
Hearts longing and chancing
A moment to be wrapped in each others charms.
There's a gentle breeze in the air
Carrying tropical exotic fragrances
Perfuming our senses
With a sweet aroma
That stirs and blurs our stares.
We're in a daze
As we gaze
Deeply into each other's hearts.
This gorgeous island garden is a magical potion
That has set into motion,
You and me
Moving closer to we.

*I was swept away by an incredible gorgeous evening in Maui.
Everything about it sounded romance.

A SUNSET

Somewhere beyond that ocean blue,
As you watch the entrance
of a colorful twilight,
You witness the sun
softly embracing the sea,
Kissing her goodnight.
You're reminded that
Far away
The gal whose lips
That would make yours stay
Forever
on hers
Is an ocean away.
So, you pray,
A wish beneath a tropic star
That she could be where you are
To hold her close
And just ummm!
Before that last breath
of romance
escapes your lips,
You sigh
a wishy dream
of some gal
Who painted upon your heart
A truly paradise place,
wherever she is
Under her loving rays,
to someday,
melt together
a sunset.

*When I use to live in Hawaii, I would often catch the most
romantic sunsets that would inspire much poetry.

TUESE C. AHKIONG

FAR AWAY FROM YOUR KISS

My eyes wake to sunny rays,
Blue-sky days,
But sadness still touches my sight,
Especially at night,
When the stars come out and play,
And remind me,
That far away,
My love lays.
Apart from my affection,
Distant from my embrace,
Somewhere beneath that blackened canopy,
How have I ever come to be,
So far away from her kiss,
I know now,
What it means
To miss.

*After a week of moving to Hawaii, these words spilled on to paper.

TUESE C. AHKIONG

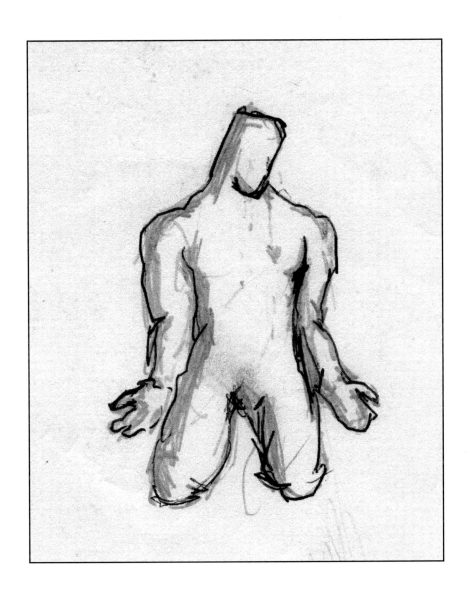

MY HOME

The days of youth
Fading to blur.
That fuzzy yesterday giggle
Moving memories stir.
Where was I when I wasn't thinking?
The past dream fallen
Dying, drowning, sinking.
Who fast-forwarded life?
Would you kindly rewind
And give me a chance to find,
Me,
And my upside down frown.
Can that smile be found?
In another ray sunned day,
Where skies aren't gray.
All around me ocean blue
Kiddies singing, dancing,
Doing what they do.
Paradise, they call this place, oooo!
It hasn't found me yet,
Nor I, it.
Here I am,
Another breath in existence.
Still waiting to live this life on pause.
If grace,
The amazing kind,
Would find, me
And lead me home.
Home,
she's out there,
Beyond where
The sky kisses the sea.
Too far away from me!
So, sing me a new tune,
One that will take away all these lonely boy blues.
The kind that curves my lips,

TUESE C. AHKIONG

That takes me on those amazing trips
Closer to you,
The very one who,
Holds my magic kiss.
So, free me from this misery.
With just one sip of your bliss,
I'd be alive again,
I'd be home.

*I had this idea that home is not just a place and building but a
person, a presence, a sigh of life.

FLOWERS TO A BOY

Your words are a gift to me,
A beautiful bouquet.
Magnificently arranged
In their colorful array.
Among the garden's
Countless many,
But not just any,
Carefully selected
For the finest,
Sweetest,
And best,
Way to express,
What's happening inside.
As you search yourself,
For those perfect words to say,
Everything you know you can't,
Put into ink,
In one moment.
Your emotions come to bloom,
And I can smell the flowers,
Perfumed in bright smiles and laughs.
Scribbled in a hug and a kiss,
The one that seals this bliss.
The part of you,
Written in sky blue,
Fragranced in springtime flowers,
I re-read for hours.
Like a favorite love song playing on repeat.
You got my dazzled eyes dancing,
Listening to your heart sing.
Moving, grooving, proving your love true.
Music as sweet as a rose,
You say I inspire what you compose?
Can anyone feel more adored than I?
Tickles me with joy.
Knowing that this boy,

TUESE C. AHKIONG

Can make your lips speak poetry,
And pull words, from your soul,
That make me,
Glow.

*There was a gal who inspired me with her words, poetry, and sighs.

THE FEELING
OF
FUNK

MAYBE

here we go again,
the thoughts are speaking to my pen.
flowing through the motions of life,
tasting another emotion,
mixed with caffeine.
contemplating, simulating, movements and plans.
will i ever be there to getta taste?
will i ever be in that place?
of enough, feeling stuffed, with content.
no situation can bring a bent to my peace.
no worries of tomorrow, hakuna matata.
no wasted sorrows,
of what hasn't been.
Today is yesterday and tomorrow not.
I should have had that extra espresso shot.
As if a stimulant can heighten my joy of reality.
It always comes down,
to the common denominator of just this.
The bliss of sweet rest goes missed.
It seems so imaginary
a dangling carrot somewhere afar, from my lips.
Eternity is in my soul
i can't understand it.
there's more to this existence
then just my 4 score and 7,
heaven?

*I scribbled this on a napkin at a coffee shop while just pondering
existence.

THE SIGHS OF LIFE

She breathes upon her lips a long lingering sigh,
Maybe of some guy, who wakes her to wonder "Am I alive?"
His words provoke her to ponder the thought "Have I caught true living?"
He tickles her mind as he exhales CO_2 in the sound of an oo
And says, "The sighs of life."
These moments in existence to know you're here;
Responding to the fragrance of the atmosphere.
It's an Interpretation that transmits the vibration of your soul;
an expression of the heart.
To know what one's spirit is feeling
By just hearing the sounds that expose
And show, with what, one's dealing.
Sighs can give the condition of your soul away.
They tell your thoughts . . .
And ask your questions, like hmmm?
These exhalations come in many sounds and flavors.
Ummm! Feeling a connecting vibe that resonates a link.
Whew! There are sighs of joyful relief,
Of completing the labors of life, receiving freedom, dodging a bullet,
Or that there's no more longing,
Just a song
because you have finally found the one to whom you belong.
There's a sweet sigh of knowing you're the one who makes your honey's eyes sparkle.
Then there are the ones of pleasure and happiness,
Ooh la la!
Feeling the sweetest highs,
That take you up to starry skies.
You're the one who makes her coo
And to sigh a breathy "I love you."
But there are also sighs that will bring you down
from the heavens to the ground;
They are ones of grief, sorrow and pain; a true disappointment.

TUESE C. AHKIONG

It's the reality of knowing you'll never have tomorrow or that appointment;
to fly away with her.
She's gone.
Or she's with another.
And so what escapes from the lips
is a depressing moan that
Sighs a groan of frustration.
Realizing your situation,
Of being
Without her.
Sigh . . .

*"The Sighs of Life" is a phrase that came off my lips back in 1998. These words summarize the many different moments in life a person comes across.

ALONE WITH A MEAL

dizzy days,
spiraling spin,
whoozy whiz,
where have I been.
let's get out of here,
the voices say,
as if the mind
could remove the frame,
it's been placed in.
even when I close the lids to objectivity,
my eyes still see hallucinogenic activity,
inside of me.
that place I thought I could be
alone.
so, with open eyes,
and mouth,
I is eating without the appetizing pleasure of conversation.
there's life going on again.
I can hear the muffled sounds of laughs,
broad-casting loud and clear
in my ear,
finding my brain
trying to entertain, me.
somewhere beneath this skull I be.
does anyone know i'm in here?
do I know if i'm in where?
I feel what I touch.
smell what I tell.
hear what I is.
think what I see.
life go by me.
right before my lips,
I desperately try to sip,
a taste beyond existence.
despair in my hair,
no shampoo care

TUESE C. AHKIONG

can do the trick
and offer this poor boy a lick
of living.
meals always go down smooth
with good conversation.

*I was studying a lot of philosophy when I wrote this.—It's not good
for man to eat alone after a philosophy class.

DESPAIR

Blanketed in darkness,
Covered in black,
On my soul gravity acts.
Pulling down to depression,
Found face ground,
Heavy my heart lays,
Silenced from its beat,
Can you make my feet,
Sing that song it once sung?
That floating free dance,
Somewhere in mid-air,
Spirals to earth,
A fallen bird,
Wingless in despair,
Drowning in the sea love,
And gasping for the very air,
That her life once supplied.
There's bad weather all around.
Stormy rain breaking inside of me.
It pours like music to my tears,
Drop, drip, plop!
Where's the heat?
The agua streams cold.
And I am alone, again.
Broken dreams stream,
Beneath the streets
Into the gutter they be.

*The end of a relationship. Nuf said!

TUESE C. AHKIONG

FUNK

another day in life
am I losing that sugar taste?
all my now and here's,
disappear.
remind me of some laugh I use to wear,
before I give into despair.
self, why be upset?
forget, regret of
I could've, would've, should've,
done my best
and know I settled for less,
and now ask
did I bite big enough?
is my experience thang stuffed?
someone quickly sing
one of those past day songs,
from the generation I belongs.
where I remember I is,
never needing to look back,
only forward to a mouth of candy smiles.
that place of sweet tooth cavities,
can anyone show me how
to dream, again?
like when I was a child I could smile
for a long while,
and not think twice
why big bird couldn't fly.
ground bound from the heavens' sky,
ain't that not strange,
here comes that wind again,
whispering,
where did life go?

*Just feeling the funk of not accomplishing goals and watching time
pass by.

MISSED

Sitting somewhere in life
watching existence transact,
i exhale another breath,
feeding the air,
as i stare,
my time going bye,
and realizing i'll soon die,
and be a forgotten name,
never to play this game,
again.
just returning as i must
to dust.
wow, how this thought holds me
kicking back, can't relax, in it's grip
knowing i'm sinking into black.
death will kiss me goodnite.
oh, golly wally, here comes that emotion.
it splashes on me like some magic potion.
there it is, right there, despair, in my hair.
back in its hand,
inescapable, incapable, of hope,
especially since there's no rope
i'm falling down
to the bottom
of no more.
ending my relation with this world
so sad and meaningless
another life goes missed . . .

*Just another funky depressing sigh of life if this physical world is
all there is. Death is so permanent and forever if there's nothing
beyond the grave.

TUESE C. AHKIONG

NOT YET, JUST EVER BECOMING

A tribute to Periclitus.

ever in the state of flux
changing not remaining
aging, raging to be
modified, never actualized
drawing near, but never here
just potential, of what isn't
becoming, not am
processing, the plan
reaching, the is
unwhere, i'm all there.

*After taking a philosophy course that mentioned Periclitus, this piece spilled from my pen.

MY PRECIOUS

Day and night, floating on my brain
in my sight, the desire to acquire
whatever shines in my eyes.
beneath the sun
a preoccupied sigh
there's only one, I think of
my precious, my immaculate,
my stuff.
those things I own
really own me.
as evening dreams breathe
my things are the featured attraction.
the star, the leading role
and there they go.
bills to the sky
always on my mind.
I hold them closely
like a man madly in love.
my every thought they possess.
My mind is flooded, occupied,
with satisfying their every monthly payment.
they are the master card.
I am their slave.
their every minimum due
is my obedient command.
supplier of my every desire,
they have all of me,
and a visa to my treasury.
Wow! The accumulation of stuff
have i got enough?
Or has it laid a bluff?
That it could satisfy, my deepest need?
let's do a discover card on my account.
oh, what do we see, greed.
The dream of the american express
lots of material things equals success.

TUESE C. AHKIONG

But at what expense: family and health?
So when I sell my soul and stuff it with things
Do they really bring, fulfillment?

*What good will it be for someone to gain the whole world, yet forfeit their soul? Or what can anyone give in exchange for their soul? Matthew 16:26

MEANINGLESS

I suppose it's that time again to ask the question
"Why or what's the meaning?"
I've seen what pleasure can bring me,
An insatiable need for more;
Acts and experiences galore,
That can never fill the emptiness inside of me.
Or how about the taste of wealth?
Men go chasing it,
Women go taking it,
Everyone is bowing down to it in worship.
My idol of gold, I've surrendered and sold,
My soul.
Yet my heart remains an empty hole.
Can knowledge satisfy?
Well, I'm sure we're gonna die!
If that is comforting to know?
What's the big deal with having a fat head,
if annihilation awaits when
you're dead.
What about the glory of fame
and popularity?
Being loved, worshipped, and
exalted by your fellow man.
Having great social status.
But that too, when old, smells
like flatus.
And leaves leaks,
As one aimlessly seeks
For that all-satisfying treasure of the soul,
That fountain of purpose,
Where one drinks
Drunk in life.
Till then . . .
"Meaningless, meaningless,
Everything is meaningless,"
The heart sighs . . .

TUESE C. AHKIONG

*In order for cries of "Meaningless, Meaningless..." to be meaningful, there must be by necessity a Mastermind behind all this. Someone who controls one's ability of coming to know The Joy of The Whole World, which would be Him. GOD, My life is in Your hands. Even my misery Has to be in Your plan. And even me contemplating these meaningful thoughts about the meaninglessness of life. ;—\

NOSTALIGIA

Amazingly, instantaneously
How a yesterday song
Can wake my memories
Spin my brain,
daze my legs
And there i am,
some time ago
Letting life flow,
some emotional Smile.
Can you smell the atmosphere?
Taste what you use to hold dear?
You go figure,
This song has done a number on me,
It's triggered history,
Those mellow yellow feelings.
Nothing more than dealing
With the sensation
Of taking a trip back in time,
The kind that rewinds
in the back of your mind.
Nostalgia, how was ya?
Where was ya?
Back then, when life was
Lighter free, in responsibilities
Brighter glee, in where will i be
Those forgotten hopes and dreams
Stream, to the surface
By a musical charm
Of what use to be.

*Every so often a song or fragrance in the air triggers some sweet
past memories.

TUESE C. AHKIONG

LIFE IS A POEM

NO MO PUBLIK ED

once upon a place,
somewhere in that space,
between the ear holes of a kindergartner,
teachers told stories
of a little girl kissin' a frog into a prince.
today, that government educated child
is herded through the university
for higher indoctrination.
sitting opened ear-ed to another storyteller,
costumed in an authoritative white coat (butcher style),
mr. professor spits out his spell
and the little sheepy follows, to slaughter, to hell.
open-minded with brains spilt-out
ms. instructor-ess has sold the fairytale again:
twice upon a time,
we were slime.
back in an hour and location no one knows,
but because I wear this lab coat it be so.
she says it started with a bang
and then a bing and then a bam!
wholy smokes mister batty-man!
from nothing, by chance,
all that you see at a glance,
came into existence!
yes! makes perfect non-sense!
it just happened,
without meaning, without purpose, you are!
you weren't meant to be.
you just exist,
for your short split moment in this,
world we call home.
earth, it feeds you to begin,
then eats you at the end.
a mad story if this is all that is meant to be.
no wonder why boys and girls aren't behavin' and playin' nice.
the masses go crazy!

TUESE C. AHKIONG

government skools teach kids they're french revolutionarily kissed
into a relative of a monkey
and dont expect them not to have problems.
if we're the illegitimate freak accident of ms. nature and mr. time
we're bond by no law.
anything goes, do as u please:
there's no right or wrong;
lie, steal, rape and kill.
poor polluted minds,
programmed for destruction.
susie, might not know howta read,
but, heck! skool has helped her to really feel good about it
with their state of the art high self-esteem programs;
compliments of the NEA regime.
johnny might not know,
that 2 and 2 b 4
but he's certainly educated and has his master's in
trojan condom mechanics and application.
government indoctrination centers preach there is no God,
do what feels good until it's over.
and why are kiddies fornicating?
-plan parent-HOOD don't u instruct them?
why are babies making babies?
-government indoctrination centers don't u show them.
why the young are illiterate?
-publik skools don't u dumb them.
why in your hallways are youth flying high without leaving the
ground?
why in your classrooms is evil like furniture hanging around?
u train these kids up in the way they should go, insane.
Save the children.
Please, no mo publik ed!
ABOLISH IT!

*I suppose one can tell I'm not so thrilled about government/ public school education. :-|
"Whoever causes one of these little ones who believe in me to sin, it would be better for him if a great millstone were hung around his neck and he were thrown into the sea." Mark 9:42

SAFE SEX

living the edge and ready to fall off.
a silly thrill promising spills.
is it hard to separate the emotion from the act of fornicating?
wishing time would rewind those days so pure.
hoping fate would deal us another hand,
but we fool ourselves again,
with that glance, ask to dance, oops! undone pants.
darling, i'll love u forever . . .
. . . tonite!
crazy how the process of rubbing the outer layer of the epidermis
cells with another has become an epidemic!
this ain't uncontrollable bodies spontaneous colliding.
this is ruthless premeditated friction.
sex today has gotten out of hand,
in fact, it's like shaking hands or saying hello.
But can u escape the emotion?
what's on the mind? what's on the heart?
both the same? or did we forget the name, already?
we can lose ourselves in that bizarre bermuda triangle,
that sea of love stuff
is always rough there.
but we don't care, we're young, strong and responsible,
government-educated, wise and invincible,
so we say, when we play—it "safe."
protect ourselves, right?
set-up those defense mechanisms,
prepare for sexual warfare:
wear the armor; use the chemical weapons
and don't let just anyone penetrate into your territory,
that's unless, we have a complete profile
on all their active missions.
but still, what good is that!
so we do some under-cover investigating,
especially when asked to do lunch? do brunch? do coffee?
do me!?
whoa, we're going a little bit too fast there!

we're not just saying "hi" and slapping hands here, lady!
this ain't no reach-out and touch someone all-over-commercial?
So, what if this is how they do it in the movies!
life aint suppose to imitate art.
adjust our minds, we are being controlled.
Media is just advertising its drug,
that adulteress-fix,
the alternative lifestyle to sooner death.
Mr. Hollywood and Ms. Plan-parenthood are both hoods, seducing
us to do the nasty.
usually for a high price too, a 10 dollar movie,
an unborn babies life!
but we don't care,
with money to spare, we dare . . .
sweeping it under the mat,
hoping it dont come back
forget the progressions, the principles,
and especially what ma and pa told us.
just run through the motions;
swim in love's oceans,
instant self-gratification
if it feels good;
Mr Nike says to "just do it"
But wait! before we go on our trip, travelin' afloat, in our sinking
boat,
don't forget our baggage;
physical, emotional, social, spiritual
-we are not immune.
who we trying to fool,
the disease has been transmitted.
there is no "safe sex",
outside of wearing a . . . .
wedding ring,
that is marriage between
-one man, one woman.
is it any wonder,
why there are no boy-girl blunders
in faithful monogamy?

TUESE C. AHKIONG

unwanted pregnancies? aids? vd?
it's pain-free,
only the sweetest ecstasies.
yet we choose to go astray and run around,
but don't we know are deeds will be found?
... and so here we are, with all of our scars.
satan, the deceiver has deceived.
we have contracted and/or conceived.
what in the world, have we believed!?
That there is no God,
we are accountable to,
therefore we can live like hell,
do what we do?
remember, we just dont do without being dunt.
God is not mocked!!
whatever we sow, we shall reap.
now, think, especially about the eternal consequences.
contrary to popular opinion
number 7, of the 10, Commandments of God Almighty
is still in full effect.
is it really worth it to play in the dark, haven't we learned,
there is no condom around the heart?
and surely not around the soul, that goes, unforgiven.
as if a thin piece of latex rubber,
could really provide any cover,
from the wrath of an angry God.

Now for the brighter note.
One that presents the antidote.
The remedy to our blues,
the good news, the cure,
the end to our death sentence,
starts in repentance
deny lucifer's lies,
turn away, from evil ways.
with God on our side,
our sins He will slay!
we can do it, because God loves us with an everlasting love.

He'll see us through it, because He desires for us to have life
abundantly,
though we have all, turned away rebelliously.
that's called sin, separation from God,
making us worthy of destruction.
apart from Him is only death,
do we not know,
God holds our next breath!?
we're dead as can be,
no good deeds, morality, philosophy, religious deeds,
can bridge the gap and set us free.
But this is what God has done!
He shows us how rich in mercy and grace He is.
Though our filthy sins make us bloody as scarlet,
He washes us white as snow.
no more shame, no more guilt;
no more sin, no more hell;
no more death.
life, through trusting faith in what Jesus Christ has done.
He has paid the ultimate price, dying our deserved penalty up there
on the cross, in our place, truly Amazing Grace.
God's undeserved favor, to make us new as can be
and give heaven free to all, we, who truly believe.

*After The Lord saved me in 1994, a fire inside of me burned to
counter the godless values I had been indoctrinated into.

TUESE C. AHKIONG

SOME PROVERBS ON SEXUAL SIN AND TEMPTATION

1. Proverbs 2:16-22 It will save you also from the adulteress, from the wayward wife with her seductive words, who has left the partner of her youth and ignored the covenant she made before God. For her house leads down to death and her paths to the spirits of the dead. None who go to her return or attain the paths of life. Thus you will walk in the ways of good men and keep to the paths of the righteous. For the upright will live in the land, and the blameless will remain in it; but the wicked will be cut off from the land, and the unfaithful will be torn from it.

2. Proverbs 5:1-23 My son, pay attention to my wisdom, listen well to my words of insight, that you may maintain discretion and your lips may preserve knowledge. For the lips of an adulteress drip honey, and her speech is smoother than oil; but in the end she is bitter as gall, sharp as a double-edged sword. Her feet go down to death; her steps lead straight to the grave. She gives no thought to the way of life; her paths are crooked, but she knows it not. Now then, my sons, listen to me; do not turn aside from what I say. Keep to a path far from her, do not go near the door of her house, lest you give your best strength to others and your years to one who is cruel, lest strangers feast on your wealth and your toil enrich another man's house. At the end of your life you will groan, when your flesh and body are spent. You will say, "How I hated discipline! How my heart spurned correction! I would not obey my teachers or listen to my instructors. I have come to the brink of utter ruin in the midst of the whole assembly." Drink water from your own cistern, running water from your own well. Should your springs overflow in the streets, your streams of water in the public squares? Let them be yours alone, never to be shared with strangers. May your fountain be blessed, and may you rejoice in the wife of your youth. A loving doe, a graceful deer— may her breasts satisfy you always, may you ever be captivated by her love. Why be captivated, my son, by an adulteress? Why embrace the bosom of another man's wife? For a man's ways are in full view of the

LORD, and he examines all his paths. The evil deeds of a wicked man ensnare him; the cords of his sin hold him fast. He will die for lack of discipline, led astray by his own great folly.

3. Proverbs 6:20-35 My son, keep your father's commands and do not forsake your mother's teaching. Bind them upon your heart forever; fasten them around your neck. When you walk, they will guide you; when you sleep, they will watch over you; when you awake, they will speak to you. For these commands are a lamp, this teaching is a light, and the corrections of discipline are the way to life, keeping you from the immoral woman, from the smooth tongue of the wayward wife. Do not lust in your heart after her beauty or let her captivate you with her eyes, for the prostitute reduces you to a loaf of bread, and the adulteress preys upon your very life. Can a man scoop fire into his lap without his clothes being burned? Can a man walk on hot coals without his feet being scorched? So is he who sleeps with another man's wife; no one who touches her will go unpunished. Men do not despise a thief if he steals to satisfy his hunger when he is starving. Yet if he is caught, he must pay sevenfold, though it costs him all the wealth of his house. But a man who commits adultery lacks judgment; whoever does so destroys himself. Blows and disgrace are his lot, and his shame will never be wiped away; for jealousy arouses a husband's fury, and he will show no mercy when he takes revenge. He will not accept any compensation; he will refuse the bribe, however great it is.

4. Proverbs 7 My son, keep my words and store up my commands within you. Keep my commands and you will live; guard my teachings as the apple of your eye. Bind them on your fingers; write them on the tablet of your heart. Say to wisdom, "You are my sister," and call understanding your kinsman; they will keep you from the adulteress, from the wayward wife with her seductive words. At the window of my house I looked out through the lattice. I saw among the simple, I noticed among the young men, a youth who lacked judgment. He was going down the street near her corner, walking along in the direction of her house at twilight, as the day was fading, as the dark of night set in. Then out came a woman to meet him, dressed like a prostitute and with crafty intent. (She is loud and defiant, her feet never stay at home; now in the street, now in the squares, at every

TUESE C. AHKIONG

corner she lurks.) She took hold of him and kissed him and with a brazen face she said: "I have fellowship offerings at home; today I fulfilled my vows. So I came out to meet you; I looked for you and have found you! I have covered my bed with colored linens from Egypt. I have perfumed my bed with myrrh, aloes and cinnamon. Come, let's drink deep of love till morning; let's enjoy ourselves with love! My husband is not at home; he has gone on a long journey. He took his purse filled with money and will not be home till full moon." With persuasive words she led him astray; she seduced him with her smooth talk. All at once he followed her like an ox going to the slaughter, like a deer stepping into a noose till an arrow pierces his liver, like a bird darting into a snare, little knowing it will cost him his life. Now then, my sons, listen to me; pay attention to what I say. Do not let your heart turn to her ways or stray into her paths. Many are the victims she has brought down; her slain are a mighty throng. Her house is a highway to the grave, leading down to the chambers of death.

5.   Proverbs 9:13-18 The woman Folly is loud; she is undisciplined and without knowledge. She sits at the door of her house, on a seat at the highest point of the city, calling out to those who pass by, who go straight on their way. "Let all who are simple come in here!" she says to those who lack judgment. "Stolen water is sweet; food eaten in secret is delicious!" But little do they know that the dead are there, that her guests are in the depths of the grave.

6.   Proverbs 22:14 The mouth of an adulteress is a deep pit; he who is under the LORD's wrath will fall into it.

7.   Proverbs 23:26-28 My son, give me your heart and let your eyes keep to my ways, for a prostitute is a deep pit and a wayward wife is a narrow well. Like a bandit she lies in wait, and multiplies the unfaithful among men.

8.   Proverbs 27:7-8 He who is full loathes honey, but to the hungry even what is bitter tastes sweet. Like a bird that strays from its nest is a man who strays from his home.

9. Proverbs 29:3 A man who loves wisdom brings joy to his father, but a companion of prostitutes squanders his wealth.

10. Proverbs 30:18-19 "There are three things that are too amazing for me, four that I do not understand: the way of an eagle in the sky, the way of a snake on a rock, the way of a ship on the high seas, and the way of a man with a maiden.

11. Proverbs 30:20 "This is the way of an adulteress: She eats and wipes her mouth and says, 'I've done nothing wrong.'

12. Proverbs 31:3 do not spend your strength on women, your vigor on those who ruin kings.

Campus club asks for student thoughts on God

Christian club offers 'God is dead' debate

By D.M. Cooney
Staff Reporter

The existence of God, the presence of evil and man's need for spiritual belief were topics addressed at an Asian American Christian Fellowship event where members sought to empower their audience with heavenly knowledge last Thursday night in Knuth Hall.

The presentation started with a video of interviews with students around campus talking about their spiritual beliefs. The responses were varied but everyone had an opinion.

"I believe God created evolution," said one student.

"I believe in a higher being but I would not use the term God," said another.

The responses from believers and non-believers included familiar themes: to deny God is to deny love; God exists in everyone and everything; I don't believe in God, evolution was a natural occurrence; I don't believe in a supreme entity - I think we are all gods.

The debate, titled "God is Dead, Evil Proves It" was the first topic of a newly formed series of "coffee talks" presented by University Fellowship and sponsored by The Asian American Christian Fellowship.

The title of the debate was derived from one of the many writings of Fredrich Nietzche, the German philosopher. Nietzche believed God was dead in the hearts of people.

"God judges man's heart. Man's ways seem innocent but God judges the motives," said Tuese Ahkiong, director of the University Fellowship and a minister of the Church of the Highlands.

Ahkiong's informal, on-campus survey questioned 121 students, staff, and faculty. Nine percent of respondants didn't know if there was a God, 14 percent said there is no God and 77 percent of those interviewed believed in some form of God or higher being.

Ahkiong's presentation about the existence of God used logic, science, history and the concept that "knowledge of God was consistent with our hearts" to reason belief in God.

Ahkiong also asked participants to explain the presence of evil in the world.

Again, a variation of responses were found; evil depends on major who declined to give his last name, said he has a strong religious background and wanted to get perspectives from others on-campus.

"I feel this is a catalyst, more exposure will make for more discussions," James said.

James said he wished there were more on-campus events that discuss philosophy and religion and said he looked forward to the next "coffee talk" panel that will be scheduled for early in the spring 2002 semester.

Don Gordon, 43, an engineer and friend of one of the fellowship members, said he attended the discussion because he was interested in the views of people on-campus.

"There is a truth out there but it is not under my control," Gordon said.

Colleen Lam, 21, a fellowship member who does not attend SF State, characterized the success of her group's first coffee talk.

"People were very excited and intrigued for our next coffee talk and that was our objective," Lam said. [X]

Contact D.M. Cooney
runbigdmcrun@netscape.net

Monica Jensen - Staff Photographer

Director of University of Fellowship Tuese C. Ahkiong presented arguments for the existence of God at Knuth Hall Thursday.

James, 19, an undeclared

SOMEWHERE IN GOD'S CREATION

Sitting somewhere in God's creation,
The moment is stilled.
My breath is taken, stolen away.
A frozen stare, but on a sunny day.
Before my eyes only the natural majesty,
Of He who created all I see,
The sky, the waters, the sand, the hand
That scribbles His praise of amazement!
Stolen away for this moment,
I am seized by the breeze of paradise.
She covers me with the breath of ocean,
Showers me with rays of warmth,
Colors my eyes skies with rainbow streaks.
Sitting on the sand with Beach earth on my feet,
Sun on my skin,
World behind my back,
A chance to gasp,
For a breath of life.
The fresh kind,
That the wind pushes from heaven,
And finds me,
laying on the ground
Floating around.
Captured by God Almighty's majesty
How can anyone ever look or see
Or even glance and say,
All this happened by chance?
When surveying the wonders of His works,
My life is halted,
To a screeching stop!
My mouth drops-
Wide opened,
eyes,
dazzled,
by the beauty shined into them.
how can I gaze across the sky

and not notice the splendor of your handiwork!?
I am trembling!
Such raw demonstration of Sovereign artistry,
all this pleasure given me.
touched by your perfect love,
inescapable, like stormy rain,
but on a clear blue day.
nothing in all creation goes untouched by your affection.
marvel of miracles,
I sit quiet still and listen to life.
Nothing is silent from offering your Name praise!
Every breath is raised to worship you!

*I wrote this back on the Waianae side of Oahu, Hawaii. I was
at a camp having a quiet time up on a mountain when God
overwhelmed me with His Glory in Creation!
" . . . Then sings my soul, my savior God to Thee, How Great Thou
Art, How Great Thou Art . . ."

I am at the University of Hawaii asking students questions about
God's existence.

TUESE C. AHKIONG

SHE LOVES HIM

she searches herself for glorious words,
to breathe, prayers, upon her lips,
like kisses, for the Lord,
covering Him, with praise, I stand amazed to be able to glimpse
into a soul and to find, the fountain
from where her passion flows.
Christ is her life.
With His glory, Her face glows it.
Everything about her new life shows it.
That she has been touched from above.
That she truly is, His beloved.
How can her speech not bless Him!?
How can her mouth not profess Him!?
And how can her tongue not confess That Jesus is Lord,
For she's covered in the Presence of God's Holy Spirit.
And her life repeatedly tells,
A sweet fragrance of words to smell,
The aroma of Christ.
Her heart beats Jesus.
It sings His Name in a song.
It tells, that it is The LORD to whom she belongs.
Indeed, she shines,
The Son, of God, brightly.
Her life story speaks of His glory.
It increases the fame of His Name.
As I listen to her adore Our Savior,
Her every last word my soul was blessed to feel.
Her prayer is pure worship of God. She is wrapped completely in
His love;
Her affection and devotion go undistracted.
With closed eyes, she smiles,
Hands praised, to the sky,
An instrument, praying,
Music to The Lord.
What a beautiful sight!
Pure and holy she stands in His light,
Just loving her King,
And knowing it brings,
Him joy . . .
She loves Him!

* I was inspired to write this poem after listening to a sister in Christ pray. Wow! Talk about a woman after God's heart!!! What a delight and gift to hear how God has blessed a life, even more so as to how God is writing out another epistle to tell the story of Jesus' glory. I love well thought out, God-centered, God-glorifying, Bible-based prayers. My discipler, Dr. Norman Luebkeman (Doc), always challenged me to think about what I pray and to not just offer up repetitious rote prayers. He told me that God loves our well thought out, biblical and beautiful prayers. I totally believe this because of the example of the Psalms. This gal made my knees weak and caused me to lift my head to see whose speaking so highly of The Lord. Of course, it's a true daughter of The King of Kings, a princess, indeed. She is worth far more than rubies. Charm is deceptive, beauty is fleeting but a woman who fears the Lord is to be praised! I always say that a woman who fears the Lord, so magnifies her beauty in every way. Words are important. I totally believe listening to a person's words reveals where their heart is. They truly speak what they value. So, too, with something as intimate as prayer, it's a powerful indicator of a person's spiritual walk and condition. I hope this poem ministers to you.

TUESE C. AHKIONG

THOUGHTS ABOUT THE END

THE GRAVE

The grave will one day eat me.
Into its mouth I will be.
6 feet beneath its gut.
Soil digesting me out its butt.
Worms and maggots feasting
On delicious Samoan Chinese cuisine.
It's hard to realize
That one day I'll fertilize
The earth I use to consume.
It does unto me,
As I did unto it.
In the end it seems,
Like we eat each others . . . uh? . . . hmmm? . . . stuff.
Stuck somewhere,
After the beginning,
And before the end.
Let's pretend it's not going to happen.
Are you ready for the ultimate thrill?
We are only a breath away from death
Inhale sustenance,
Exhale death.
Life flowing forward,
Unwinding thru time,
Spiraling downward,
Where nobody will find,
That person behind the name.
As if he's still there.
Not even the soul remains.
That thing that occupied body thru space.
Its planet flesh suit disintegrates
Biodegrades.
Eternity lies before our eyes.
Open wide to ultimate reality.
We exercise futility,
For our brief moments,
Under the sun

As we wait for oblivion
To eat us.
That's if there is no one
Beyond the grave.

*Just some thoughts of a living man about the great and awesome
event each person has a date with, death.

THE SHORTNESS OF LIFE

youth deceives,
the mature conceives,
old age believes,
annihilation.
here today,
gone someday,
sooner than yesterday
been dying since my birthday.
death, she comes for us all.
we know not the hour
but our date with destiny is set.
our secret rendevouz will be met,
as we near closer to the grave,
when we'll embrace,
a chance,
to dance.
take a dip
then slip,
from life.
silly romantic twist,
literally takes my breath away,
especially, when she shuts off the lights,
whispers in my ear,
"I'll take you somewhere you've never been!"
then she takes me!
upon my lips hers lay.
I close my eyes from sight no more.
she steals the kiss of life from this boy!
lousy date!
a vapor of passion,
kills without compassion.
don't you just hate poems that have to rhyme!
anyhow, give me some time to find
the kind of words I can voice
about the shortness of life,
or what about the length of Death

that thing that takes away every breath.
she stands ready each second,
to crush the living into the dead.
she hunts us down,
and we will be f . . . . located
discriminate of none,
an equal opportunist,
prepared to kill,
the weak, the ill,
whoever it wishes,
its goodbye kisses.
no more hi's,
it's time to die.
and if the grave is all that awaits us,
let us eat, drink, be merry,
for tomorrow we die.
short,
wasn't it!
life . . .

*This is dedicated to all the living waiting in line to die. Seek The Lord while you still have breath and while He still may by found as Savior and not a Consuming Fire.

TUESE C. AHKIONG

SCRIPTURE ON THE BREVITY AND MEANINGLESSNESS OF LIFE APART FROM GOD

. . ."Naked I came from my mother's womb, and naked I will depart. The LORD gave and the LORD has taken away; may the name of the LORD be praised."

"Man born of woman is of few days and full of trouble. He springs up like a flower and withers away; like a fleeting shadow, he does not endure. Do you fix your eye on such a one? Will you bring him before you for judgment? Who can bring what is pure from the impure? No one! Man's days are determined; You have decreed the number of his months and have set limits he cannot exceed. So look away from him and let him alone, till he has put in his time like a hired man.

If it were his intention and he withdrew his spirit and breath, all mankind would perish together and man would return to the dust.

"LORD, make me to know my end And what is the extent of my days; Let me know how transient I am. "Behold, You have made my days as handbreadths, And my lifetime as nothing in Your sight; Surely every man at his best is a mere breath. Selah. "Surely every man walks about as a phantom; Surely they make an uproar for nothing; He amasses riches and does not know who will gather them.

What man can live and not see death, or save himself from the power of the grave? Selah

You turn men back to dust, saying, "Return to dust, O sons of men." For a thousand years in your sight are like a day that has just gone by, or like a watch in the night. You sweep men away in the sleep of death; they are like the new grass of the morning—though in the morning it springs up new, by evening it is dry and withered. We are consumed by your anger and terrified by your indignation. You have set our iniquities before you, our secret sins in the light of your presence. All our days pass away under your wrath; we finish our years with a moan. The length of our days is seventy years— or eighty, if we have the strength; yet their span is but trouble and sorrow, for they quickly pass, and we fly away. Who knows the power of your anger? For your wrath is as great as the fear that is due you. TEACH US TO NUMBER OUR DAYS ARIGHT, THAT WE MAY GAIN A HEART OF WISDOM.

For He knows how we are formed, he remembers that we are dust. As for man, his days are like grass, he flourishes like a flower of the field; the wind blows aover it and it is gone, and its place remembers it no more.

When you hide your face, they are terrified; when you take away their breath, they die and return to the dust.

your eyes saw my unformed body. All the days ordained for me were written in your book before one of them came to be.

Man is like a breath; his days are like a fleeting shadow.

Now listen, you who say, "Today or tomorrow we will go to this or that city, spend a year there, carry on business and make money." 14Why, you do not even know what will happen tomorrow. What is your life? You are a mist that appears for a little while and then vanishes.

"Meaningless! Meaningless!" says the Teacher. "Utterly meaningless! Everything is meaningless." I have seen all the things that are done under the sun; all of them are meaningless, a chasing after the wind.

. . . I wanted to see what was worthwhile for men to do under heaven during the few days of their lives.

Then I turned my thoughts to consider wisdom, and also madness and folly. What more can the king's successor do than what has already been done?

I saw that wisdom is better than folly, just as light is better than darkness.

The wise man has eyes in his head, while the fool walks in the darkness; but I came to realize that the same fate overtakes them both.

Then I thought in my heart, "The fate of the fool will overtake me also. What then do I gain by being wise?" I said in my heart, "This too is meaningless."

For the wise man, like the fool, will not be long remembered; in days to come both will be forgotten. Like the fool, the wise man too must die!

So I hated life, because the work that is done under the sun was grievous to me. All of it is meaningless, a chasing after the wind. I hated all the things I had toiled for under the sun, because I must leave them to the one who comes after me. And who knows whether he will be a wise man or a fool? Yet he will have control over all the work into which I have poured my effort and skill under the sun. This too is meaningless. So my heart began to despair over all my toilsome labor under the sun. For a man may do his work with wisdom, knowledge and skill, and then he must leave all he owns to someone who has not worked for it. This too is meaningless and a great misfortune. What does a man get for all the toil and anxious striving with which he labors under the sun? All his days his work is pain and grief; even at night his mind does not rest. This too is meaningless.

There is a time for everything, and a season for every activity under heaven: a time to be born and a time to die

I also thought, "As for men, God tests them so that they may see that they are like the animals. Man's fate is like that of the animals; the same fate awaits them both: As one dies, so dies the other. All have the same breath ; man has no advantage over the animal. Everything is meaningless. All go to the same place; all come from dust, and to dust all return. Who knows if the spirit of man rises upward and if the spirit of the animal goes down into the earth?"

Naked a man comes from his mother's womb, and as he comes, so he departs. He takes nothing from his labor that he can carry in his hand.

This too is a grievous evil: As a man comes, so he departs, and what does he gain, since he toils for the wind?

Then I realized that it is good and proper for a man to eat and drink, and to find satisfaction in his toilsome labor under the sun during the few days of life God has given him—for this is his lot.

A man may have a hundred children and live many years; yet no matter how long he lives, if he cannot enjoy his prosperity and does not receive proper burial, I say that a stillborn child is better off than he. It comes without meaning, it departs in darkness, and in darkness its name is shrouded. Though it never saw the sun or knew anything, it has more rest than does that man—even if he lives a thousand years twice over but fails to enjoy his prosperity. Do not all go to the same place?

For who knows what is good for a man in life, during the few and meaningless days he passes through like a shadow? Who can tell him what will happen under the sun after he is gone?

It is better to go to a house of mourning than to go to a house of feasting, for death is the destiny of every man; the living should take this to heart.

When times are good, be happy; but when times are bad, consider: God has made the one as well as the other. Therefore, a man cannot discover anything about his future.

In this meaningless life of mine I have seen both of these: a righteous man perishing in his righteousness, and a wicked man living long in his wickedness.

Since no man knows the future, who can tell him what is to come? No man has power over the wind to contain it; so no one has power over the day of his death.

All share a common destiny—the righteous and the wicked, the good and the bad, . . .
As it is with the good man, so with the sinner; . . .
This is the evil in everything that happens under the sun: The same destiny overtakes all. The hearts of men, moreover, are full of evil and there is madness in their hearts while they live, and afterward they join the dead. Anyone who is among the living has hope—even a live dog is better off than a dead lion!
For the living know that they will die, but the dead know nothing; they have no further reward, and even the memory of them is forgotten. Their love, their hate and their jealousy have long since vanished; never again will they have a part in anything that happens under the sun.
Enjoy life with your wife, whom you love, all the days of this meaningless life that God has given you under the sun— all your meaningless days. For this is your lot in life and in your toilsome labor under the sun. Whatever your hand finds to do, do it with all your might, for in the grave, where you are going, there is neither working nor planning nor knowledge nor wisdom.

Moreover, no man knows when his hour will come: As fish are caught in a cruel net, or birds are taken in a snare, so men are trapped by evil times that fall unexpectedly upon them.

As you do not know the path of the wind, or how the body is formed in a mother's womb, so you cannot understand the work of God, the Maker of all things.

However many years a man may live, let him enjoy them all. But let him remember the days of darkness, for they will be many. Everything to come is meaningless.

Remember your Creator in the days of your youth, before the days of trouble come and the years approach when you will say, "I find no pleasure in them"—before the sun and the light and the moon and the stars grow dark, and the clouds return after the rain; when the keepers of the house tremble, and the strong men stoop, when the grinders cease because they are few, and those looking through the windows grow dim; when the doors to the street are closed and the sound of grinding fades; when men rise up at the sound of birds, but all their songs grow faint; when men are afraid of heights and of dangers in the streets; when the almond tree blossoms and the grasshopper drags himself along and desire no longer is stirred. Then man goes to his eternal home and mourners go about the streets. Remember Him—before the silver cord is severed, or the golden bowl is broken; before the pitcher is shattered at the spring, or the wheel broken at the well, and the dust returns to the ground it came from, and the spirit returns to God who gave it. "Meaningless! Meaningless!" says the Teacher. "Everything is meaningless!"

Now all has been heard; here is the conclusion of the matter: Fear God and keep his commandments, for this is the whole duty of man. For God will bring every deed into judgment, including every hidden thing, whether it is good or evil.

And he told them a parable, saying, "The land of a rich man produced plentifully, and he thought to himself, 'What shall I do, for I have nowhere to store my crops?' And he said, 'I will do this: I will tear down my barns and build larger ones, and there I will store all my grain and my goods. And I will say to my soul, Soul, you have ample goods laid up for many years; relax, eat, drink, be merry.' But God said to him, 'Fool! This night your soul is required of you, and the things you have prepared, whose will they be?' "This is how it will be with anyone who stores up things for himself but is not rich toward God."

Unless the LORD builds the house, its builders labor in vain. Unless the LORD watches over the city, the watchmen stand guard in vain. In vain you rise early and stay up late, toiling for food to eat—for he grants sleep to those he loves.

Job 1:21; 14:1-6; 34:14-15, Psalm 39:4-6; 89.48; 90:3-12; 103:14-16; 104:29; 139:16; 144.4; James 4:13-14, Ecclesiastes 1:2, 14; 2:3, 12-23; 3:1-2, 18-21; 5:15-16, 18; 6:3-6, 12; 7:2, 14-15; 8:7-8; 9:2-10, 12; 11:5, 8; 12:1-8, 13-14; Luke 12:16-21; Psalm 127:1-2

TUESE C. AHKIONG

GOD IS MY SONG-PASSAGES

The LORD is my strength and my song; he has become my salvation. He is my God, and I will praise him, my father's God, and I will exalt him.

The LORD is my strength and my shield; my heart trusts in him, and I am helped. My heart leaps for joy and I will give thanks to him in song.

By day the LORD directs his love, at night his song is with me— a prayer to the God of my life.

The LORD is my strength and my song; he has become my salvation.

Surely God is my salvation; I will trust and not be afraid. The LORD, the LORD, is my strength and my song; he has become my salvation."

Exodus 15:2; Psalm 28:7; 42:8; 118:14; Isaiah 12:2

I WISH YOU WERE MY GIRL

Ever since I met you, .
I'm always thinking of you
Ever since I met you,
all my thoughts are you.
Whenever you're near me
My temperature starts rising
Whenever it's you I see
I get the chills and my heart pounding.

I wish you were my girl, oooh
I wish you were my girl, oooh

It would be special,
if you thought of me
It would be magic,
if I was your dream.
Your sweetness makes me weak,
I'm gaga and cannot speak
Your beauty takes my breath away,
I'm choked up, but want to say . . .

I wish you were my girl, oooh
I wish you were my girl, oooh

BRIDGE-instrumental

I can't, get to bed
You're always running through my head
I can't, get you off my mind.
I'm dreaming of you all the time.
Your hand in mine,
would be Ooooh, Ahhhh
Your lips on mine
Ooooh, Ahhhh
I want you to want me
I'm wishing that you're wishing

TUESE C. AHKIONG

I was your man.
I want you to want me
I'm wishing that you're wishing
I was your man.

I wish you were my girl, oooh
I wish you were my girl, oooh

I can't, get to bed
You're always running through my head
I can't, get you off my mind.
I'm dreaming of you all the time.
Your hand in mine,
would be Ooooh, Ahhhh
Your lips on mine
Ooooh, Ahhhh
I want you to want me
I'm wishing that you're wishing
I was your man.
I want you to want me
I'm wishing that you're wishing
I was your man.

Ooh, Ahh, Ooh, Ahh,

I wish you were my girl, oooh
I wish you were my girl, oooh
I wish you were my girl, oooh
I wish you were my girl, oooh

*This song has taken years to finish. Back in 2005, I was jamming
with a good friend, Brad Toyama in his car along with his wife and
her friend. He was playing cords on his uke and I was just throwing
down different words and out came, "your hand in mine, would
be Ooooh, Ahhh, Your lips on mine, Ooooh, Ahhh." It wasn't until
2010 that the rest of the lyrics started to flow, especially since I was
motivated to write this book and include this song in it.

I SAVED MY HEART FOR YOU

Before this day had come
We waited patiently
Pure and faithfully
Now I can sing to thee
I saved my heart for you
I saved my heart for you

When you walked into my life
Heaven sent you
I knew you'd be my wife
Today it comes true
I saved my heart for you
I saved my heart for you

Singleness I won't miss
Seal our love with a kiss
A miracle has been done
Two hearts now beat as one

On our wedding day,
Bells will be ringing
Family, friends and we,
All will be singing
I saved my heart for you
Nobody else but you
Can't wait to say I do

I saved my heart
I saved my heart
I saved my heart
I saved my heart
For you.

*In 1998, Brad and I wanted to write a song for our friend, Owen's wedding. Brad again was just jamming random cords and I came up with these lyrics.

TUESE C. AHKIONG

DREAMIN' WITH MY EYES OPEN

Sweet dreams, are all I ask of you
Cuz when I sleep, that's all I want to do.
I say a prayer, to the Lord up above,
That you'd be there, to give me all your love.
I hope to see,you in my dreams,
I know you're all, I'll ever ever need.
Our dreams can take, us anywhere,
My darling will, I see you there.

With you, i'm dreamin' with my eyes open saying words i've never
spoken-2x

Goodnite my love, I'm off to sleep,
A rendevouz, I hope you'll keep.
I'll wait for you, Until it's light,
So meet me in, my dreams tonite.
I close my eyes, and there you are.
I feel you near, tho' you are far.
And when I wake, girl please be there,
your life, your love, I long to share.

With you, i'm dreamin' with my eyes open saying words i've never
spoken-2x

I'm dreamin', That your love is here
Dreamin'-that you want me near
I'm wishin', That you'd soon would find
Wishin', That your love was mine
I'm hopin', That when you look at me
Hopin', That you'll say and see.

With you, i'm dreamin' with my eyes open saying words i've never
spoken-2x

*This is the third song that I was able to pen shortly after the wave
of excitement from writing my first.

STROLLIN' WITH MY BABY

I want to go strollin' with my baby. Strollin' with my baby

Strollin' with my baby
Holding hands
Such a great feeling between
A girl and her man.
Maybe to the beach,
A park or shoppin' mall?
Doesn't matter which
Because we'll do them all.

I want to go strollin' with my baby. Strollin' with my baby

Walking arm and arm snuggled up together,
We'll stay closely tight
No matter what the weather.
Cruisin' down a street,
A road or avenue,
We'll be happy singin',
Baby I love you.

I want to go strollin' with my baby
Strollin' with my baby

Strollin' with my baby, strollin' with my baby, strollin' with my baby,
strollin'-2x

Strollin'-down main street
Strollin'-with my only sweet
Strollin'—to a lover's beat
Strollin' —with happy feet

Moving side by side, we get closer each step.
Love is ever growing since the day that we met.
I'll stay right beside you every step that we take.
Happy ever after is the love that we'll make.

TUESE C. AHKIONG

I want to go strollin' with my baby
Strollin' with my baby

*As a teen, I loved listening to my sister Tina and cousins sing "So much in love" acappella. I later formed an acappella group and sung this song as one of our repertoire. The song sings about strolling and inspired me to write my own strolling song. I always thought there was something special about simply strolling with the one you love.

YOU ARE MY BABY

you are my girl and I am your man.
I love you so why can't you understand.
there's no reason to doubt me,
no reason can't you see.

cuz you, you are my baby
you, you are my baby
and i'll be true to you.
only you, no one else, only you in my heart.

when i'm away from you, I feel so sad
I need you next to me, or else i'll go mad
you're never far, from my thoughts
if you're not here, I know i'll be lost.

cuz you, you are my baby
you, you are my baby
and i'll be true to you.
only you, no one else, only you in my heart.

believe me when I say
you're in my thoughts everyday
you're such a special girl
I just want to be in your world.

when we're together I need to know
that you're going to love me and you'll never go
you're so precious, so sweet
girl, why can't you see-

that you, you are my baby
you, you are my baby
and i'll be true to you.
only you, no one else, only you in my heart.

*After writing my first song, "Happy Birthday Baby" back in 1990, I was excited about writing more songs and came up with "You are my baby." My musical influence has come from 50s, 60s, 70s oldies, R&B, doowop, and acappella.

DEEPER

Deeper, I am falling, I'm falling in love, I'm following for you.
Deeper, I am falling, I'm falling in love, I'm following for you.

All my life, living without you
Just getting by, no one to come home to.
I don't know, where I've been,
But since I met you, I started to live.

Deeper, I am falling, I'm falling in love, I'm following for you.
Deeper, I am falling, I'm falling in love, I'm following for you.

The Lord says, it's not good,
to be all alone, just by yourself.
Now you're here, I've found my home
Happy in love, Lonely days are gone.

Bridge-instrumental

You're the best thing, That's happened to me
Your sweetness and love, Makes my heart sing
You're the gal, I've been waiting for
The one I love, And will forever adore.

Deeper, I am falling, I'm falling in love, I'm following for you.
Deeper, I am falling, I'm falling in love, I'm following for you.

*Brad and I were jamming on the uke back in 1998 and I was able
to come up with the refrain. We thought it was going to be a praise
song but when I started working on it again for inclusion in this
book, it turned into a love song.

TUESE C. AHKIONG

YOU'RE THE LORD OF MY LIFE

You're the Lord of my Life, Lord of my Life.
Lord of my Life, Lord of my Life.

Ever since you found me, Lord
My Life has become new.
You turned my heart from darkness To the beauty found in You.
You have rescued my soul.
Freed me from my sin.
Filled my life to over flow,
Yes! I'm born again!

You're the Lord of my Life, Lord of my Life.
Lord of my Life, Lord of my Life.

I am bought, at a precious price
for me to live is honoring Jesus Christ.
To die is gain, making His glory known,
To worship Him,ever before His throne.

You're the Lord of my Life, Lord of my Life.
Lord of my Life, Lord of my Life.

Jesus, You are, My life, my hope, my strength, My everything.
Jesus, You are, My life, my hope, my strength, My everything.
I live for you alone, to bring glory to your throne 2x

To do your will and serve you, Lord, that is my very food
To increase the fame, of your name, is what I want to do.
So, fill me, Lord, with your power, and move me to proclaim
your amazing grace, your endless love, the glory of your reign.

You're the Lord of my Life, Lord of my Life.
Lord of my Life, Lord of my Life.

*I wrote this song back in the Summer of 2005. At the time, I
remember studying God's Sovereign Grace in saving my lost
undeserving and wicked soul. I recall just being so grateful to praise
My Lord with this song. For months, I would begin and close each
the day praising my Lord with this song. ;-)

LORD, YOU MAKE MY HEART SING

Lord you make my heart sing (echo)
You opened up my eyes to see (echo)
Your love, How it showers on me.
Lord you make my heart sing (echo)
You opened up my eyes to see (echo)
Your love, How it showers on me.

Amazing Grace
How you took my place
On the cross
To save a lost
Soul like me
So I could see
Your love

Lord you make my heart sing (echo)
You saved me from my misery (echo)
By your blood, How it covers O'er me
Lord you make my heart sing (echo)
You saved me from my misery (echo)
By your blood, How it covers O'er me.

*I remember having these lyrics and melody in my head. After coming to Brad, he easily found the cords to make this song sing praises to The Lord.

TUESE'S TESTIMONY

Have you ever been misled? I was misled to as a boy. I grew up in a very religious home where we did a lot of religious stuff. I was told if I kept all the religious rules of the church and did good, I would be in right standing with the priest, God and have a happy life. What a lie! I started reading the Bible for myself and saw how this religion contradicted its teaching. I was exposed to a perverted priest (He's lucky he didn't try anything physical with me.). I also saw many hypocrisies in what the religious adults taught compared to the Bible. Many adults I was exposed to were alcoholics, adulterers, womanizers, wife-beaters, gamblers, child abusers, drug users, convicts, thugs, etc, etc.

So, I rejected the Roman Catholic religion and became a pagan. I lived for pleasure, status and stuff. I was a good heathen by the world's standards. I was blessed with the ability to knock people out, so, I became a boxer. I represented the USA in international competition; won the National Golden Gloves; 7x state champion; and 5x Golden Glove Champion. Unfortunately, I went to CCSF and SFSU and got my mind fried and polluted by the Humanists, naturalists, evolutionists, atheists, moral relativists, sexual perverts, and New Age Occultists who were my teachers. While in college, I had a "mi vida loca" episode in that I was living a Tuese gone wild and crazy existence.

In October of 93, I was on a boxing trip to Texas, when I was divinely appointed to room with Dr. Norman Luebkeman (Doc), an official judge. It was divine because of the conflict of interest of a judge rooming with an athlete. Doc befriended me and over the course of a year through his life and love, he introduced me to Christ. I knew of Jesus at a young age but didn't personally know Him. I lived as a civilized sinner hiding most of my sins from the public radar. I did many things I'm ashamed of. I thought by satisfying all my self-centered desires, I would be fulfilled. I was dead wrong! I was still empty as can be, until God made this blind man see, that the God-shaped vacuum in me, could only be filled by He. I tried filling myself with partying, accomplishments, girlfriends, titles, philosophies/religions, knowledge, good deeds and money. Those things didn't work. They left me empty. The vanity and futility of life: we're born, we fiddle around for x amount of years and then we perish. "Meaningless, meaningless, all is meaningless, a chasing after the wind." Just like Mick Jagger said, I, too, couldn't get no satisfaction! I found myself asking the ultimate questions of life: What is Truth? What's the meaning of life? Why am I here? How should I live? Where did I come from? Does God or gods exist? Where am I going when I die?—If we're all just accidents, then life is ultimately a meaningless race towards oblivion and annihilation. In fact, like the song says, we're living in oblivion.

Doc shared with me The Gospel, which means "Good News." It's Good News because there's some serious Bad News. This is the simple message that totally changed my life:
A loving God continually blesses us. As ungrateful creatures (sinners), we rebel (sin) against Him. So righteous judgment awaits us all (This is the Bad News). But God has made a promise of Grace (a gift; unmerited, undeserved, unearned favor). Christ accomplished undeserved salvation for sinners. To be saved one must believe upon Jesus. The Holy Spirit enables a person to come to Jesus. Those who are saved lead new lives.

This word, "grace" opened heaven to me. I grew up thinking that to be right with God, I had to be a good religious person. This is totally wrong. Heaven is a gift that Jesus Christ purchased with His shed blood on the cross for His people and is received by grace through faith.— "Amazing grace how sweet the sound that saved a wretch like me. I once was lost but now I'm found, was blind but now I see." Grace means undeserved, unmerited, unearned favor/gift of God. It is God who grants this gift of grace to whomsoever He chooses.

"For it is by grace you have been saved, through faith—and this not from yourselves, it is the gift of God— not by works, so that no one can boast. For we are God's workmanship, created in Christ Jesus to do good works, which God prepared in advance for us to do."
Ephesians 2:8-10

TUESE C. AHKIONG

In September of 1994, I shared with Doc that I wanted to be closer to God. He smiled and said he believed that the Holy Spirit had touched my life. We prayed. I repented of my sins and trusted Jesus with all my heart. I remember feeling a powerful cleansing deep within my soul. It was like an ocean flood of God's love, peace, purpose and joy pouring into me. I felt so clean as if I had never done anything wrong and experienced a joy I had never tasted. That day powerfully confirmed in my spirit that I belonged to the Lord. Life hasn't been the same since! And it hasn't been a bed of roses either. Life is sweet with The Lord in it, but it's war in many other ways.

After being rescued, I found a great community of believers with whom I grew in the Faith. I turned into an avid reader of Scripture and Christian literature (theology, apologetics, philosophy, discipleship-Christian living) in that you couldn't find me without a book. My car became a seminary in that I had Christian radio booming all the time. After a few years, I felt led to become a missionary, so I went to suffer for the Kingdom in 80-degree tropical heat and on white sandy beaches in Hawaii from 1997-2000. Hehehe! ;-P Remember, there's another side to paradise that is dark and evil.—Anyhow, that is where I received my Jedi training in ministry; my faith was like on steroids out there in that I grew so much.

I returned in 2000 and was ordained as a Christian Minister/Teacher at a Chrisitain School in San Bruno as a Bible, P.E., Math and teacher/coach. So, I'm spoiled because I get to teach little ones about Jesus and big ones, too, and the Lord provides. I also serve in Jail ministry at the 850 Bryant's—Hall of Justice and lead a Christian ministry, called ARM: Always Ready Ministries. It specializes in Discipleship, Evangelism and Apologetics among youth, college and adults. Teaching, defending and proclaiming the Gospel is my passion.—I so desire to seek God's Kingdom, Righteousness and the mission I believe He has given me and that is "To know Jesus Christ and to make Him known."

If you know The Lord as The Rescuer of your soul and Master of your life, then I hope my testimony has been encouraging. If you do not know The Lord Jesus Christ as your Savior and King, it is my prayer that He would grant you His amazing grace and the gift of His Holy Spirit.

GOD IS THE AUTHOR OF MY FAITH, NEW LIFE AND DESTINY VERSES

1. **1 Peter 1:3-4** Blessed be the **God and Father** of our Lord Jesus Christ, **who according to His great mercy has caused us to be born again** to a living hope through the resurrection of Jesus Christ from the dead, to obtain an inheritance which is imperishable and undefiled and will not fade away, reserved in heaven for you,

2. **1 Cor 1:24,30-31** but to those whom God has called, both Jews and Greeks, Christ the power of God and the wisdom of God . . . **It is because of him that you are in Christ Jesus,** who has become for us wisdom from God—that is, our righteousness, holiness and redemption. Therefore, as it is written: "Let him who boasts boast in the Lord."

3. **2 Cor 5:17-18** Therefore, **if anyone is in Christ,** he is a new creation; the old has gone, the new has come! **All this is from God, who reconciled us to himself** through Christ and gave us the ministry of reconciliation:

4. **Eph 1:4-5 For he chose us in him before the creation of the world** to be holy and blameless in his sight. **In love** 5he predestined us to be adopted as his sons through Jesus Christ, in accordance with his pleasure and will—

5. **Eph 1:11 In him we were also chosen, having been predestined according to the plan** of him who works out everything in conformity with the purpose of his will,

6. **1 Thess 5:9** For **God did not appoint** us to suffer wrath but **to receive salvation** through our Lord Jesus Christ.

7. **2 Thess 2:13-14** "But we should always give thanks to God for you, brethren beloved by the Lord, because **God has chosen you from the beginning for salvation** through sanctification by the Spirit and faith in the truth. And it was for this He called you through our gospel, that you may gain the glory of our Lord Jesus Christ."

8. **2 Tim 1:9** who has saved us and called us to a holy life not because of anything we have done but because of his own purpose and

TUESE C. AHKIONG

grace. **This grace was given us in Christ Jesus before the beginning of time,**

9. **Deut.7:6-8** "For you are a holy people to the Lord your God; the Lord your <u>God has chosen you</u> to be a people for Himself, a **special treasure** above all the peoples on the face of the earth. <u>"The Lord did not set His love on you nor choose you because you were more in number than any other people, for you were the least of all peoples; "but because the Lord loves you, and because He would keep the oath which He swore to your fathers, the Lord has brought you out with a mighty hand, and redeemed you from the house of bondage, from the hand of Pharaoh king of Egypt.</u>

10. **Deut 10:14-15** "Behold, to the LORD your God belong heaven and the highest heavens, the earth and all that is in it. "Yet on your fathers did the LORD <u>set His affection to love them</u>, and He <u>chose</u> their descendants after them, <u>even you above all peoples</u>, as it is this day.

11. **Deut 30:6** <u>The LORD your God</u> will circumcise your hearts and the hearts of your descendants, <u>so **that you may love him** with all your heart and with all your soul, and live.</u>

12. **Psalm 37:39** <u>The salvation of the righteous **comes from the LORD;**</u> he is their stronghold in time of trouble.

13. **Psalm 65:4** How blessed is the one whom **You choose** and bring near to You To dwell in Your courts We will be satisfied with the goodness of Your house, Your holy temple.

14. **Eze 36:26-27** "Moreover, **I will give you a new heart and put a new spirit within you**; and <u>I will remove the heart of stone from your flesh and **give you a heart of flesh**. "I will put My Spirit within you and **cause you** to walk in My statutes</u>, and you will be careful to observe My ordinances.

15. **Jer. 24:7,** "'And <u>**I will give them a heart to know Me**</u>, for I am the Lord; and they will be My people, and I will be their God, for they will return to Me with their whole heart."

16. **1 Cor 12:3** Therefore I tell you that no one who **is** speaking by the Spirit of God says, "Jesus be cursed," and **no one can say, "Jesus is Lord," except by the Holy Spirit.**

17. **Jonah 2:9** But I will sacrifice to You With the voice of thanksgiving That which I have vowed I will pay **Salvation is from the LORD."**
18. **Matt 1:21** She will give birth to a son, and you are to give him the name Jesus, because **he will save his people from their sins."**
19. **Matt 11:27** "All things have been handed over to Me by My Father; and no one <u>knows</u> the Son except the Father; nor does anyone <u>know</u> the Father except the Son, and <u>anyone to whom</u> **the Son wills to reveal Him.**
20. **Matt 19:25-26** When the disciples heard this, they were greatly astonished and asked, "<u>Who then can be saved?</u>" Jesus looked at them and said, "**With man this is impossible, but with God all things are possible."**
21. **John 1:12-13** But as many as received Him, to them He gave the right to become_children of God, even to those who believe in His name, **who were born,** not of blood nor of the will of the flesh nor of the will of man, <u>but **of God**</u>
22. **John 3:3-8** In reply Jesus declared, "I tell you the truth, no one can see the kingdom of God unless he is **born again."** "How can a man be born when he is old?" Nicodemus asked. "Surely he cannot enter a second time into his mother's womb to be born!" Jesus answered, "I tell you the truth, no one can enter the kingdom of God <u>unless he is born of water and the Spirit.</u> Flesh gives birth to flesh, but the Spirit gives birth to spirit. You should not be surprised at my saying, 'You must be **born again.'** <u>The wind blows wherever it pleases. You hear its sound, but you cannot tell where it comes from or where it is going. So it is with everyone</u> **born of the Spirit."**
23. **Acts 11:18** When they heard this, they had no further objections and praised God, saying, "<u>So then, God has</u> **granted even the Gentiles repentance unto life."**
24. **2 Tim 2:24-26** And the Lord's servant must not quarrel; instead, he must be kind to everyone, able to teach, not resentful. 25Those who oppose him he must gently instruct, <u>in the hope that God will</u> **grant them repentance** <u>leading them to a knowledge of the truth,</u> 26and that they will come to their senses and escape from the trap of the devil, who has taken them captive to do his will.

TUESE C. AHKIONG

25. **Phil 1:29** For <u>**it has been granted**</u> <u>to you on behalf of Christ not</u> <u>only</u> **to believe on him**, but also to suffer for him,

26. **Acts 13:48** When the Gentiles heard this, they were glad and honored the word of the Lord; <u>and all who</u> **were appointed for eternal life believed.**

27. **Acts 16:14** "... Lydia, from the city of Thyatira, a seller of purple fabrics, a worshiper of God, was listening; and **the Lord opened her heart** <u>to respond to the things spoken by Paul."</u>

28. **Acts 18:27** ... those who had **believed through grace,**

29. **John 5:21.** "For just as the Father raises the dead and gives them life, even so the **Son also gives life to whom He wishes.**

30. **John 6:37-39** <u>All that the Father gives me will come to me</u>, and whoever comes to me I will never drive away. For I have come down from heaven not to do my will but to do the will of him who sent me. And this is <u>the will of him who sent me, that</u> **I shall lose none of all that he has given me,** but raise them up at the last day.

31. **John 6:44** "**No one can come to me unless the Father who sent me draws him**, and I will raise him up at the last day."

32. **John 6:64-65** Yet there are some of you who do not believe." For Jesus had known from the beginning which of them did not believe and who would betray him. He went on to say<u>, "This is why I told you that</u> **no one can come to me unless the Father has enabled him."**

33. **John 10:11** "I am the good shepherd; the good shepherd lays down His life <u>for the sheep."</u>

34. **John 10:24-29** The Jews gathered around him, saying, "How long will you keep us in suspense? If you are the Christ, tell us plainly." Jesus answered, "I did tell you, but you do not believe. The miracles I do in my Father's name speak for me, but <u>you do not believe because</u> **you are not my sheep. My sheep** <u>listen to my voice; I know them, and they follow me.</u> **I give them eternal life**, <u>and they shall never perish; no one can snatch them out of my hand. My Father, who has given them to me, is greater than all; no one can snatch them out of my Father's hand.</u> 30I and the Father are one."

35. **John 17:2** For you granted him authority over all people that <u>he might</u> **give eternal life to all those you have given him.**

36. **John 17:6** "I have revealed you **to those whom you gave me out of the world**. They were yours; you gave them to me and they have obeyed your word.

37. **Eph5:25** Husbands, love your wives, just as <u>Christ loved **the church** and gave himself up for **her**</u>

38. **Rom 1:6-7** And **you also are among those who are called to belong to Jesus Christ. To all in Rome who are loved by God and called to be saints:** Grace and peace to you from God our Father and from the Lord Jesus Christ.

39. **Heb12:2** Let us fix our eyes on Jesus,**the author and perfecter of our faith,**who for the joy set before him endured the cross, scorning its shame, and sat down at the right hand of the throne of God.

40. **Gal 1:15-16** But when God, who **set me apart from birth and called me by his grace**, . . .

41. **Jude** 1Jude, a bond-servant of Jesus Christ, and brother of James, **To those who are the called, beloved in God** the Father, and kept for Jesus Christ:

42. **Rom 8:28-30** And we know that God causes all things to work together for good <u>to **those who love God**, to those who are **called** according to His **purpose**</u>. For those whom He **foreknew**, He also **predestined** to become conformed to the image of His Son, so that He would be the firstborn among many brethren; and these whom He **predestined**, He also **called**; and these whom He called, He also **justified**; and these whom He justified, He also **glorified.**

43. **Rom 11:2-7** God did not reject his people, **whom he foreknew.** Don't you know what the Scripture says in the passage about Elijah—how he appealed to God against Israel: "Lord, they have killed your prophets and torn down your altars; I am the only one left, and they are trying to kill me"? And what was God's answer to him? "I have **reserved** for myself seven thousand who have not bowed the knee to Baal." So too, at the present time there is a remnant **chosen by grace**. And <u>if by grace, then it is no longer by works; if it were, grace would no longer be grace</u>. What then? What Israel sought so earnestly it did not obtain, but **the elect** did. The others were hardened,

TUESE C. AHKIONG

44. **Titus 3:5** <u>he saved us</u>, not because of righteous things we had done, but **because of his mercy**. He saved us through the washing of rebirth and renewal by the Holy Spirit,

45. **1 Peter 2:8-9** and, "A STONE OF STUMBLING AND A ROCK OF OFFENSE"; for they stumble because they are disobedient to the word, and to this doom they were also <u>appointed</u>. But you are A **<u>CHOSEN RACE</u>**, A royal PRIESTHOOD, A HOLY NATION, A PEOPLE FOR God's OWN POSSESSION, so that you may proclaim the excellencies of **Him who has called you out of darkness into His marvelous light;**

46. **1 John 4:10** In this is love, not that <u>we</u> have loved God but that <u>He loved</u> **us** and sent his Son to be the propitiation <u>for</u> **our** <u>sins.</u>

47. **Rev 13:8** All who dwell on the earth will worship him, everyone whose <u>name has not been written from</u> **the foundation of the world in the book of life** <u>of the Lamb</u> who has been slain.

48. **Isaiah 53:11** Out of the anguish of his soul he shall see and be satisfied; by his knowledge shall the righteous one, my servant, **make many** <u>to be accounted righteous, and he shall bear their iniquities.</u>

49. **Matt 20:23**. He said to them, "My cup you shall drink; but to sit on My right and on My left, this is not Mine to give, but <u>it is for those for whom it has been **prepared** by My Father.</u>"

50. **Luke 2:14** "Glory to God in the highest, and on earth <u>peace to men on whom his favor rests.</u>"

51. **1Jn 4:19** We love Him, because <u>He first loved us</u>"

TUESE'S BIO

Tuese Ahkiong is a man of faith in Jesus Christ. He has been an ordained Christian minister/ teacher in San Bruno, California from 2000 to the present, 2011. He has an A.A. from C.C.S.F. and a B.S. from Excelsior College in Liberal Studies. Prior to teaching he was a missionary with Hawaii Youth For Christ from 1997-2000. Ahkiong is the director of ARM: Always Ready Ministries, a discipleship, evangelism and apologetic ministry.

At a young age, Ahkiong demonstrated exceptional athletic skills. He was a 2-time San Francisco All-City Football Running Back. He also succeeded in "the art of boxing," as he likes to call it, in becoming the U.S. National Golden Gloves Super Heavy Weight Champion (98); 3-time U.S. National Bronze Medalist (85, 94, 2000); 7-time state champion (5-time State Golden Glove Champion (94, 96, 98, 99, 2000), Junior Olympic State Champion (85), ABF State Champion (2000)). His successes in boxing enabled him to share his testimony and story with thousands of young people.

Tuese has a variety of interests and hobbies. He enjoys singing, cooking, martial-arts, hiking, dancing (salsa, cha cha, swing, hip hop), photography, creating and playing group games, philosophizing, Disc Jockeying weddings and parties as DJ 2e, and especially, teaching God's Word to youth and adults.

Another avenue Ahkiong expresses himself in is the sportswear market. He trademarked the name, "THE M.A.N., Modeled After None." It is Ahkiong's desire to direct his company to create positive images and messages to permeate the atmosphere. THE M.A.N. stands for excellence.

THE
M.A.N.
MODELED AFTER NONE

"The Spoken Word Slamma Jamma" is an open mic event Tuese created back in 1999. The name is not to be associated with "poetry slams where people are in verbal battle" but "poetry showcases." It's just a catchy title pulled out of his bag. He wanted a venue where people could display their creative skills and enjoy a time of music, fun, games, and artistic expressions. The experience itself of "The Spoken Word Slamma Jamma" would be its own artwork as observers would compose together an evening of creativity. He hosts The Spoken Word Slamma Jamma's every few months at local coffee shops, books stores, churches, colleges, and dessert parlors like Sweet Connections. ;-)

TUESE C. AHKIONG

Creative expression became a passion to let his soul flow as he was seeing poetry everywhere. He started immersing himself with other hearts in different streams of expression: dance, guitar, acappella music, song composition, graphics, drawing, t-shirts . . . and BOOM: The Spoken Word Slamma Jamma!!!

Come and get your fix and taste the dancing of souls in the collective smorgasborg of creative expression. If you are interested in seeing Tuese as well as others recite and perform their works live or on video, contact Tuese at tuese.ahkiong@gmail.com.

Life is a poem.

Enjoy your sighs of life.

TUESE C. AHKIONG